J577

Renfrewshire
Council

LW

The library is always open at
renfrewshirelibraries.co.uk

Visit now for
homework help
and free
eBooks.

SKOOBS

We are the Skoobs and we love the library!

Phone: 0300 300 1188
Email: libraries@renfrewshire.gov.uk

Crabs, Dabs and Rockpools

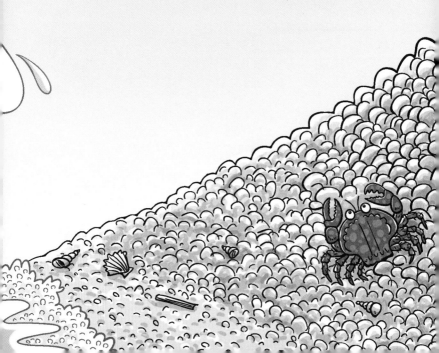

Crabs, Dabs and Rockpools

Written and illustrated by
TONY DE SAULLES

Orion
Children's Books

ORION CHILDREN'S BOOKS

First published in Great Britain in 2016
by Hodder and Stoughton

1 3 5 7 9 10 8 6 4 2

Text and illustrations © Tony De Saulles 2016

A CIP catalogue record for this book
is available from the British Library.

ISBN 978 1 4440 1550 8

Printed and bound in China

The paper and board used in this book are from well-managed
forests and other responsible sources.

Orion Children's Books
An imprint of
Hachette Children's Group
Part of Hodder and Stoughton
Carmelite House
50 Victoria Embankment
London EC4Y 0DZ

An Hachette UK Company
www.hachette.co.uk

www.hachettechildrens.co.uk

For Ava,
when you next visit the beach at Troon

RENFREWSHIRE COUNCIL	
198364021	
Bertrams	19/07/2016
577.699	£4.99
LIN	

CONTENTS

1
A day on the beach

It is high tide and the waves are big.

We will have to wait for low tide when the sand appears and it is easier to explore the rocks and pools. Incredible creatures are waiting to be discovered!

At high tide the sea washes all sorts of interesting things onto the beach. It is fun to search for treasures in the high tide line.

You might find a piece of driftwood
worn smooth by the sea, cuttlefish bones,
dead jellyfish and crabs or bits of rope
and buoys from fishing boats.

Above the high tide line you find special plants that only grow by the sea.

After the tide has reached its highest point, the sea drops back and slowly uncovers the beach. Trapped seawater makes pools in the hollows of rocks.

Are there creatures living in
these rock pools?

Let's take a look.

2
Rock pool life

Rock pools are full of life.
But they are dangerous places
for small rock pool creatures.

When you first peer into a rock pool
your shadow and movement will frighten
the animals down below. They will hide
under rocks and in the sand.

But wait quietly for a few minutes
and the creatures will appear.

Crabs are happy in and out of the water.

A crab's shell protects it from danger
like a knight's armour.

As a crab grows, its shell becomes tighter and tighter until it pops off. But don't worry, it has a new shell underneath!

Prawns have clever ways to avoid being eaten. They can spot danger with their amazing eyes on movable stalks and swim fast to escape.

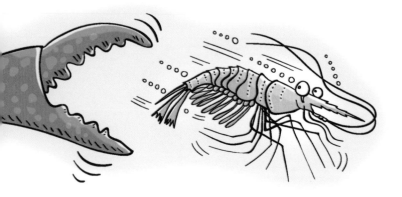

Their see-through bodies blend in with the background making it hard for hungry fish to see them.

The **starfish** is an incredible creature!
The tips of its arms can sense light and
help it to see where it's going.

Starfish have lots of tiny feet for holding
onto rocks and moving about.

If a starfish loses an arm it can grow
another and the cut off arm will grow
more arms to become a new starfish!

The sea is full of tiny young sea animals and other small algae plants and creatures called **plankton**. Plankton is an important food for some of the creatures in this book.

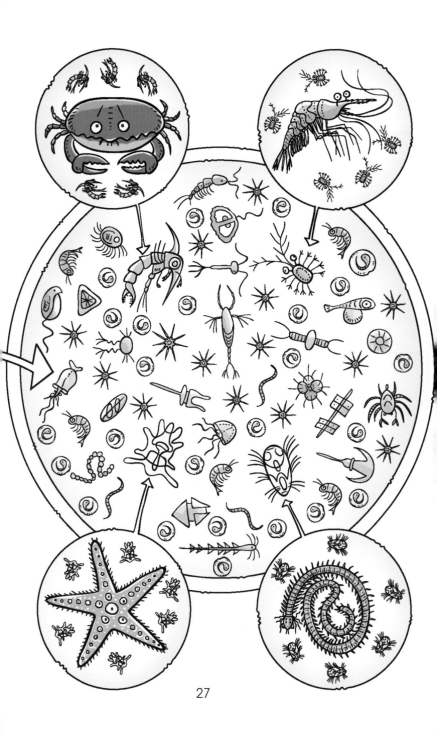

The **shanny** eats tiny crabs and shrimps
and has special fins for climbing out
of one rock pool and into another.
It can even change colour to blend in
with its surroundings.

Hermit crabs make their homes in empty seashells. When they grow too big for their borrowed home, they move to a bigger one.

3
On the rocks

Not all beach creatures live in rock pools at low tide. Some have to survive out of water.

Imagine your house filling with water twice a day. It would be horrible!

But beach creatures have clever ways
to survive high tides and low tides.
At low tide, the crabs, worms and shellfish
that haven't found a pool, keep cool and
damp by hiding under rocks and seaweed.

Mussels are shellfish that also live on rocks and shut tightly at low tide to avoid being eaten.

Barnacles look like shellfish but actually belong to the same family as crabs and prawns.

At high tide, mussels and barnacles open and feed on plankton.

Limpets clamp tightly onto rocks
and wait for the sea to cover them.
Under water, they slide about feeding
on algae but they always return
to the same spot!

These shiny red blobs are **beadlet anemones**. Under water they catch small fish by stinging them with their poisonous tentacles.

Lift a rock or seaweed near the high tide line and you might see some **sea slaters**. They hide in the damp and come out at night to feed on dead plants and animals.

Sea slaters are from the same family as woodlice, little creatures that live under the rocks in your garden.

Did you know that some seaweeds can
be cooked to make a tasty dinner?

4
Hiding in the sand

Let's jump down from the rocks
and look at the sand.

It is the power of the sea that creates sandy beaches. Crashing waves smash into cliffs and wear them down into pebbles and sand.

Under the sea, powerful currents and tides drag rocks over the seabed and grind them into sand.

Winter storms stir the sand and pebbles up from the sea and spit them out onto beaches.

The wind blows lighter grains of sand up the beach to make **sand dunes**.

Marram grass, with its tangle of roots, stops sand dunes from blowing away.

Sand hoppers feed at night on rotting seaweed in the high tide line.

If you could hop as high as a sand hopper you would be able to jump over your house!

Down by the water, **ragworms** crawl over sand and seaweed hunting for food. They have strong jaws that shoot out to grab small beach creatures.

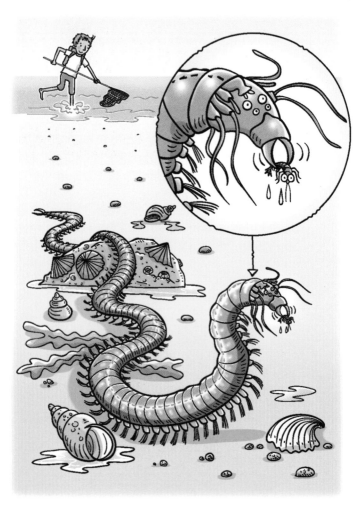

These wiggly piles of sand are made by **lugworms**. Lugworms feed by swallowing sand that contains tiny bits of food. They get rid of the sand by pumping it out of their bottoms like toothpaste from a tube!

The creatures living in these muddy brown
tubes are called **peacock worms**.

When you see them under water you'll understand how they got their name.

Like beautiful peacock feathers!

Dabs are flatfish that blend in with the sandy seabed. Because they live on the bottom of the sea they have both eyes on top of their head!

Say hello to my flatfish relatives!

sole

flounder

plaice

Cockles and **razor shells** hide
under the sand.

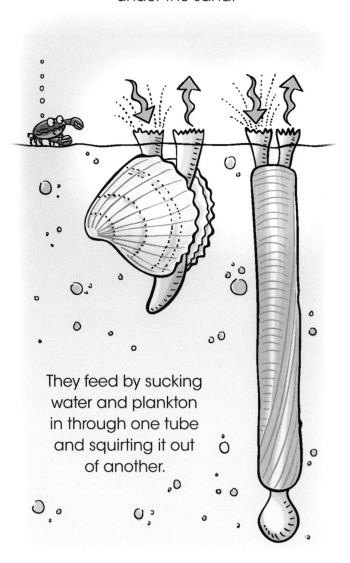

They feed by sucking
water and plankton
in through one tube
and squirting it out
of another.

But even under the sand shellfish are not always safe. Hungry humans and seabirds are looking for their dinner.

5
Dinosaur rocks

Fish, crabs, shellfish and starfish have
lived in the sea for millions of years.
We know this because of fossils.

When animals die they usually rot
and dissolve back into the ground.
But sometimes, when an animal dies in
the right sort of place, a fossil is made.

This is the fossil of an **ammonite**.

Ammonites were swimming in the sea
millions of years ago but they died out like
the dinosaurs. They are extinct.

But how did the ammonite turn into a fossil?

When the ammonite died it sank down into the muddy seabed.

The soft parts rotted away and mud covered the hard shell.

Over millions of years the mud and the ammonite turned into stone.

When the softer rock that was mud is broken open, the hard ammonite fossil is found inside.

Fossil hunters have also found fossils of plants and insects and dinosaurs.

You can be a fossil collector too.
On some beaches you will find extinct
creatures like ammonites or maybe the
fossil of a beach creature that is
still around today.

Things to do

Building a
sandcastle

drawing pictures
in the sand

beach combing

body boarding

rockpooling

swimming

spotting beach
creatures

fossil and shell collecting

skimming stones

WHAT WILL YOU

Dive into the deep dark sea.

Come face to face with incredible dinosaurs.

DISCOVER NEXT?

Take a look at your own back garden.

Speed off to outer space.

It's never too early to find out more.